LifeC
Jimi
A Biography

By Lora Greene

BookCaps™ Study Guides
www.bookcaps.com

© 2014. All Rights Reserved.

Cover Image © micky333 - Fotolia.com.

Table of Contents

ABOUT LIFECAPS..3

CHAPTER 1: CHILDHOOD AND EARLY YEARS...5

CHAPTER 2: MILITARY SERVICE............................**17**

CHAPTER 3: EARLY MUSICAL CAREER **22**

CHAPTER 4: THE JIMI HENDRIX EXPERIENCE ..**34**

CHAPTER 5: WOODSTOCK **59**

CHAPTER 6: BAND OF GYPSYS **65**

CHAPTER 7: CRY OF LOVE TOUR **70**

CHAPTER 8: ELECTRIC LADY STUDIOS **74**

CHAPTER 9: EUROPEAN TOUR **76**

CHAPTER 10: LEGACY **83**

WORKS CITED **86**

About LifeCaps

LifeCaps is an imprint of BookCaps™ Study Guides. With each book, a lesser known or sometimes forgotten life is recapped. We publish a wide array of topics (from baseball and music to literature and philosophy), so check our growing catalogue regularly (**www.bookcaps.com**) to see our newest books.

In the world of classic rock, there is one name that nearly everyone has heard: Jimi Hendrix. A genius on the electric guitar, Jimi Hendrix singlehandedly revolutionized the world of music with his talent, his attitude, and his personality. He inspired musicians and people not only in the United States, but also across the world.

He was a star in the 1960s and the 1970s, rocking out on blues, jazz, soul, and rock music. He collaborated with many other musicians, and also did some solo works that were huge successes. His music remains popular today because of the effect it had on the world; he worked during a very turbulent era in America's history.

In this book, you will read about the man, the myth, the legend Jimi Hendrix, whose memory lives on in his spectacular music.

Chapter 1: Childhood and Early Years

The name "Jimi Hendrix" is well-known, but many people do not know his original birth name. His father and mother named him Johnny Allen Hendrix. He was born in 1942, three years before the end of World War II, on November 27th.

His father's name was James Allen Hendrix, although he typically went by "Al." His mother's name was Lucille Hendrix. The two of them lived in Seattle, Washington. Together, they had five children, and Johnny Allen was the oldest of them. The Hendrix family was not very rich; Al Hendrix moved from job to job, never able to find the right place. He was a dancer, and loved to dance to jazz, the most popular genre during the time.

When Al Hendrix realized that finding a job was too difficult, he decided to join the United States Army. He was sent from Seattle, Washington to Fort Sill, Oklahoma, a journey that lasted 2,000 miles. Al Hendrix was sent overseas to France to fight Germany. When the war ended in 1945, he came home a changed man. He decided that he was going to rename his eldest son, so he changed Johnny Allen's name to James Marshall Hendrix. "James" would later become "Jimi."

Life at the Hendrix household was not the same when Al came back from World War II. Al and Lucille fought much more often; ultimately, they decided that there was no path other than divorce. If the divorce was not enough, both Al and Lucille wanted custody over the children. They went to court to decide.

Lucille liked to drink a lot, which was a deciding factor in the courts. Al Hendrix was given custody of the five children. Young James Marshall missed his mother dearly, and rarely saw her again. Now, he lived with his father Al, his two sisters Kathy and Pamela, and his two brothers Leon and Joseph.

He was a great student in school; he went to the local Washington Junior High School and received excellent grades. Many historians credit his high school days as some of the most important in forming his musical talents and interest. His high school was very diverse, and he had friends of all cultures and races: Europeans, Asians, and Africans were all a part of his life. This is important because jazz and blues are two genres that emerged from early African music. His knowledge of other cultures helped him write music that could appeal to all people.

Age fifteen was an important year in the life of James Marshall Hendrix. First of all, it was the year that he lost his mother forever. While he had rarely seen her after his parents' divorce six years earlier, he still loved thinking about his mother. To him, his mother was a very important figure in his life. Unfortunately, his mother died in 1958 due to her heavy drinking.

By the time she entered the hospital, it had been months since he had last met with his mother, or even talked to her. Al told him that his mother had been remarried, however, to a man named William Mitchell. But it was not long after her remarriage that fell she ill with *hepatitis*, a condition in which your liver swells and inflames. This most likely happened because she drank too much alcohol, and alcohol damages your liver.

Jimi's aunt, Dolores, knew that Lucille's kids needed to see her before she died. Jimi visited his mother in the hospital, which made him very glad. After a few days, the doctors released Lucille from the hospital, believing she would be okay. Unfortunately, not too long after, Lucille collapsed outside a bar and died. Her spleen had ruptured.

Jimi was absolutely devastated. He believed that his mother might actually survive. Al took Jimi and his brothers to the funeral home, but they were not allowed to see their mother's body because they were far too young, Al thought. Jimi sat in his father's truck while Al went inside the funeral home and said his final farewell to his ex-wife. When the official funeral took place, Al refused to attend, something that made Jimi and his brothers very angry. Jimi even said, years later, that he never forgave his father for that.

Something extraordinary happened in the same year that Lucille passed away — something that would change James and the world forever. From one of his father's friends, he paid five dollars for an acoustic guitar. He had never taken lessons before, and had just about no idea how to play it. But he was drawn to the guitar nevertheless; he imagined himself playing before crowds, so that is what he set out to do.

He went to the store and purchased records so that he could listen to the way that certain players used their guitar. He watched his friends and other performers so that he could imitate their playing style.

One of his favorite musicians to watch was the famous Elvis Presley; during the 1950s, Elvis shook the world with his rock and roll music. Audiences had never heard such excellent music, or even seen the way that Elvis shook his hips and danced on stage. While some people believed that Elvis was wildly inappropriate, others screamed and cried if they got the chance to see him at a concert. Elvis went on to earn a prestigious title, The King of Rock and Roll. Jimi Hendrix especially idolized Elvis. He loved Elvis's music, but more than that he liked the passion and enthusiasm that Elvis showed on stage. Later in life, when Jimi was asked about what he thought of Elvis growing up, he replied, "Man, they were cool. They made music seem like the best thing in the world." And to Jimi, it was.

After his mother's death, Jimi had many strong emotions. He was angry and sad and upset all at the same time, and he used music to help him cope. He poured all of his emotion into his music, and it made him feel much better.

Jimi's schoolwork and grades suffered, though. He would often skip class so that he could visit other musicians, and he was constantly thinking about his guitar during class. He wanted nothing more than to skip school, play his guitar, and make good music. At the end of his freshman year of high school in 1958, he received some bad news: he needed to stay back one year. He would be a freshman once again, since his grades had been so poor.

Staying back hardly helped him. He still found it hard to concentrate. It wasn't only his music, but he and his father kept switching apartments. Al was having trouble finding good jobs, and his money was hard to come by. Jimi even needed to change schools, since his father moved to a different area.

Despite all of this trouble, Al did something for Jimi that was spectacular: he purchased a white electric guitar, his first non-acoustic instrument. But if you have an electric guitar, you also need an amplifier, which is a speaker that you can connect the guitar to. It helps the guitar play louder, since electric guitars are typically used in rock bands with loud drums and other guitars. He also did not have a case for his guitar, which protects it. He decided he was going to ask around the neighborhood, and see who would be willing to make some music.

Learning the electric guitar was slow at first. He played everything note by note, starting with small lines, then whole songs. Eventually, he could play almost anything, and even make some songs up. He found some neighborhood kids to jam with for a little while, and he even played some songs with his dad, who was trying to learn the saxophone. Because of his hard work and his neverending persistence, Jimi entered his first band.

They were called the Velvetones. He saw an advertisement for an audition, and immediately decided to try out. They played jazz and R&B (also known as rhythm and blues). There were some much more experienced members in the band, and Jimi thought it was a great opportunity to play with other people. The Velvetones asked around town to see which clubs they could play at, and they got a yes from Birdland, a popular club.

During their gigs at Birdland, Jimi would take solos on the guitar, some that lasted ten minutes long. People that watched him for the first time remember that his playing was "wild." People had never heard music like that before; Jimi jammed out, throwing out crazy notes and screeching riffs. People tried to dance to it, but they found that it was so unusual that they could do little else but watch in awe.

This is something that instantly makes Jimi Hendrix a genius. Throughout musical history, the biggest success stories come from musicians that go against the status quo. Even the greatest classical composers, like Mozart and Beethoven, tried out and composed new music that was unusual for the time. For this reason, people were interested in their music and always wanted to hear more. Jimi's new way of playing was so strange and unique, that people could not help but stop and listen to him.

Jimi's dad Al had a recent change of heart about Jimi's playing. He thought it was so unusual that it was inappropriate. He would never force Jimi to stop playing guitar, but he made it quite clear that he was not happy with the way Jimi's music was going. This hurt Jimi, coming from the man that bought him his first electric guitar. Many of Jimi's friends later said that Jimi kept his guitar at a friend's house because he was afraid his father would find it and get rid of it.

Jimi soon left the Velvetones and joined another Seattle band, called the Rocking Kings. They played blues and jazz as well, but they also played rock, one of Jimi's favorite genres of music. The Rocking Kings wanted people to dance, to always keep the party going. It was when Jimi joined the Rocking Kings that something horrible happened.

After an event one night, Jimi accidentally left his guitar backstage. When he went back to get it the day after, it was gone. He asked all the management in the building, and none of them had seen it. Jimi realized that his guitar had been stolen, and what was even more terrifying was the thought of breaking the news to his father.

Jimi stalled the news, always telling his father that he forgot his guitar at a friend's house. One day, his dad told him to bring his guitar home, and that's when Jimi broke. He revealed that his special electric guitar had been stolen. Al, of course, was upset. He told Jimi, "You're gonna have to do without a guitar for a while." The Hendrix family just did not have the money to invest in another guitar.

When Jimi went to his fellow band members in the Rocking Kings and broke the bad news, they instantly understood. They didn't want Jimi to be without a guitar, so they all pooled their money and got Jimi a new guitar! It cost $50 in 1959; in today's money, that would be nearly $400! It's a good thing that Jimi got a new guitar, because the Rocking Kings would go on to do some awesome gigs. They played in the Seattle Seafair Festival, and also competed in Washington's Battle of the Bands, achieving second place.

While all of this was happening, Jimi's school life was plummeting further and further downhill. His highest grade was a B (in art), and he was failing almost all of his other classes. The school allowed him to continue to 11th grade, but he would not stay in his junior year for long. After two months, he made the decision to drop out of high school.

He now had to be a fulltime musician, despite the fact that his father and family was upset at this decision. For some side money (playing small gigs at bars hardly brought Jimi any good salary), his father wanted Jimi to help with some landscaping jobs; his father had been hired by a landscaping company, and loved it. The same, though, could not be said for Jimi, who found the work to be horribly boring. Even worse, his father was not willing to pay him that much. Jimi decided that he would much rather direct his energies towards music, no matter what the pay.

During one day at the landscaping company, Jimi got into a furious fight with his father. Years later, reflecting on the job, Jimi said that "I had to carry stones and cement all day and [my dad] pocketed the money . . . I ran away after a blazing row with my dad. He hit me on the race and I ran away." Things would only get more difficult for Jimi.

In the meantime, he had a girlfriend named Betty Jean. He was so infatuated with her that he thought about marrying her, despite the fact that they were young and Jimi did not have a great job. When he proposed to her, she thought he was joking. Both she and her parents just laughed, because the idea was so ridiculous.

In the next few months, Jimi would be caught riding in two stolen cars. He was a troubled kid. He never wanted to commit crimes, but somehow it just ended up happening. Still suffering from emotional trauma from the death of his mother, Jimi had to deal with a poor home life, the guilt from dropping out of school, and trying to reach a musical career that seemed to be failing before his very eyes. When he was put into jail, his father immediately bailed him out. After that, he went to court and tried to rethink his life. And that was when he thought of the United States Army.

Chapter 2: Military Service

During the 1950s and 1960s, racial discrimination was alive and well in the United States. In the south, white and black children went to different schools, different restrooms, were not allowed to sit next to each other on the bus, drank from different water fountains, and more. Many employers did not want to hire African-Americans, partially because they might have been racist themselves. Either way, Jimi knew that it was hard enough to get a job. So the army seemed like the perfect place to go.

During his court case, Jimi said that he would join the army if his punishment was not so severe for stealing two cars. The courts agreed. It was decided: Jimi Hendrix would join the army.

The day after the court hearing, he registered for a three year term. As with many people that join the army, he was incredibly nervous. Years later, he recalled, "I sat on the bed and had a little talk with myself. It might have been the first time I was thinking as a man, not a dumb kid. I made myself a kind of promise—Don't look back. If you do, it will hold you back." Jimi was growing up, and this experience in the United States Army would change his life.

Before he left for the Army, he played one last performance with his band, and he also met with Betty Jean. Even if he had not taken his last marriage proposal seriously, he decided he would give it another shot. He slipped a rhinestone ring onto her finger, considering it an engagement ring.

On May 31st, 1961, Jimi Hendrix arrived in the town of Fort Ord, California for his training. The first step was basic training, which involved numerous physical and disciplinary exercises that Jimi did well at. Over the course of the next few weeks, he thought often about his father, Betty Jean, and his hometown. But most of all, he thought about his guitar. It was the thing he simply could not live without. After sending a letter to his father, asking for it, Al shipped it to Fort Ord.

The next step in the Army came as an assignment. Jimi was to travel to Fort Campbell in the state of Kentucky; there, he would work for the 101st Airborne Division. And if this was to be his assignment, he would need to learn how to parachute.

The parachute training was fun, as one can imagine. Jimi was so good at the training that he received a special award, called the Screaming Eagle Patch. He was very proud of himself for earning it; ever since he had found about the award in Fort Ord, California, he had wanted to earn it. And he had.

But it still was not the highlight of Jimi's time in the Army. It was his guitar. Once people at Fort Campbell learned that Jimi was a very talented musician, they came by to stop and listen to him play. He received compliments from all around. With one of his friends at Fort Campbell, whose name was Billy Cox, he started a small band with five members. During the week, they would practice with any free time they were given. During the weekend, they would go to clubs on the army base and play. None of the other musicians were too talented when it came to singing, so Jimi took lead vocals; after all, he had done some singing gigs during his time with the Rocking Kings.

Jimi Hendrix and Billy Cox decided that they needed to name their band; they eventually came up with the Kasuals, and they became popular on the army base. Soon, people in North Carolina were asking for the Kasuals to come and play for them.

But that's when things in the Army started to go downhill. At the time, the United States was fighting a very violent war in the Asian country of Vietnam. Vietnam was split in half; North Vietnam was a communist country, which America disliked. They thought that if Vietnam became entirely communist, then other countries would become communist too, and the U.S. saw this as a threat. Communism is a form of government made most popular by the Soviet Union, the former government of Russia. South Vietnam was supported by the United States, because they wanted to have a democracy. When North and South Vietnam were at each other's throats, America entered the war to help out the South. Vietnam was a very unpopular war, because many people believe the United States had no business interfering in other countries' politics. Nevertheless, it remains as one of the most horrific and deadly wars to date. Approximately 59,000 American soldiers perished; an example of senseless tragedy at the hands of politics.

When Jimi was training in the Army, things in Vietnam were escalating from bad to worse. The American president, Dwight D. Eisenhower, and his successor John F. Kennedy, only seemed to be willing to send more soldiers into Vietnam. As you can imagine, Jimi was frightened. He did not want to shipped anywhere. He knew that he needed a way out of the Army; he still had two years left in his Army term, and he could be sent to Vietnam at anytime.

He went to the doctor on the base, and said that he was homosexual, or gay. In today's world, more people are accepting of gay rights and marriage. But during the 1950s and 1960s, it was outlawed. Today, we are beginning to accept gay men and women in the military. But in Jimi Hendrix's time, you could be sent home from the military for being gay. Jimi told the doctor he was starting to become attracted to his male colleagues. In addition to this, he claimed that he was having trouble sleeping at night, he was dizzy and nauseous, his chest hurt, and he was losing weight too quickly. The doctor decided that it was a hazard to Jimi's health, and the men around him, for him to remain in the military. Hence, Jimi was discharged and returned home.

Chapter 3: Early Musical Career

When Jimi arrived home, the first thing people wanted to know was how he was able to skip military service — especially since his agreement to military service had been a big part of his court trial months earlier. When friends and family asked, he concocted a lie that he had broken his ankle during parachute training. He did not want anyone to think that he might be gay, or that he was lying about being gay to get out of the military — it was seen as a shameful act of cowardice. However, we know now that he never broke his ankle. Records from the military never say anything about a broken ankle, but they do have files about Jimi claiming to be homosexual.

He instantly returned to playing at gigs with his friends in the Kasuals. When he served in the Army, he was allowed a certain amount of "leave" time, meaning that he could go home or take a small vacation off duty. However, he did not use all of this leave time. Because he had extra, the Army gave Jimi money to make up for the time he spent on base. He received four hundred dollars, but it did not last long. In fact, it lasted one night. He walked into a bar in Clarksville and was so happy to be free from the military that he volunteered to pay for everyone's drinks in the bar. At the end of the night, there were sixteen dollars left in his pocket.

This meant, clearly, that he would not be able to make the trip from Clarksville back home to Seattle. It was simply too expensive. Instead, he decided to get an apartment in Clarksville with his friend Billy Cox and a girl he met named Joyce. He realized he needed to break the news to Betty Jean, that he would not be able to come home. Betty Jean was so upset that she put her engagement ring in an envelope and sent it to Jimi.

Jimi was heartbroken, but it seemed that he and Betty Jean just weren't meant to be, since they were practically half a world apart and there was so much between them. Jimi decided to focus on his life and his musical career. He and Billy Cox entered another Battle of the Bands competition in Indianapolis, since they had scored so well in their previous competition. Once again, they got second place.

It was on this night that Jimi Hendrix's next band was formed. At the Battle of the Bands, a guitarist named Alphonso Young was amazed by the Kasuals' talent, and he wanted to join. Along with him was a singer named Harry Batchelor. They were instantly allowed into the band, which they soon renamed the King Kasuals.

Together, the King Kasuals played at clubs in Tennessee at least twice a week—they were popular too! They knew the best music, and they knew what people wanted to dance too. Because of this, they had a great following. And who wouldn't want to see Jimi Hendrix play? His name was slowly becoming well known.

But despite this popularity, Jimi still knew he had much more to learn. There were a million guitarists out there better than him, and another million bands that could beat them in a competition. Jimi continued to talk to every guitarist he met; he absorbed their advice like a sponge, taking in every word. He practiced every single day, and sometimes he could hardly sleep at night because he was itching to grab his guitar and practice some more. Even if you don't like Jimi Hendrix's music, you have to admit that his dedication and commitment to music is nothing less than admirable.

Sometimes, though, despite his enthusiasm, he still failed. On a stage once, he tried to have a guitar duel (like a musical battle, with solos!) with a man named Johnny Jones, one of the most talented guitar players of the time. It went horribly, and Jimi Hendrix was practically laughed off the stage. This event fueled his desire to learn even more, but it also got him down in the blues. When he called his father to get support, his father made him "feel like a failure," as Jimi once said.

He left the King Kasuals and moved to Vancouver, which was where his grandmother Nora was living. For the next few months, he bounced between a few bands, never seeming to find his niche. He never gave up practice, though. He knew he was going to make it one day; he just needed to keep up his practice and his motivation.

He thought that he might find his big break in the Big Apple, the city where dreams came to fruition: New York City. Jimi Hendrix left his grandmother's house and took a bus to New York, with only his guitar and a single bag. When he arrived in the city, he expected to be graciously handed great gigs.

His dream was far different from the truth. Instead of finding a city with countless opportunities, he found a city that was too big, with too many people, too many clubs, and most of all, too many expectations. He went to the Harlem area, made popular thirty years earlier during a time period called the *Harlem Renaissance*. This was a time period during the 1920s and 1930s, in which many African-Americans flocked to the Harlem area and made great bounds in music, art, literature, and thought. Jazz was popular in Harlem and, even though Jimi Hendrix liked jazz, he liked rock and roll more.

The people of Harlem, though, did not like rock and roll. In fact, when you played at a club or any other event, you were *expected* to play some form of jazz, whether it be blues or R&B. Jimi was intimidated at first, but he was determined to make it big in the Big Apple.

As with many things in life, Jimi was not immediately successful. It took perseverance, and he had it. He moved from place to place, having several different roommates. He played with different bands and gained plenty of experience along the way.

The next summer took him away from New York, through Kansas City, and into the heart of Atlanta where he met a man named Little Richard. At the time, Little Richard was known for his incredible rock and roll music: he was a national hit. When he got the opportunity to join Little Richard's band, the Upsetters, there was no way he could turn it down. Little did he know that he wouldn't have the greatest time with them.

For one thing, the Upsetters were pretty strict on regulations. Everyone had to follow a dress code if they performed on stage; they did not want any of their members to look casual, whereas Jimi Hendrix dug the casual look. No one in the band was allowed to *improvise*, or make up music as they go along, usually in the form of a solo while the rest of the band plays background music. This was because Little Richard did not want anyone to seem better than him.

Eventually, Jimi Hendrix became so upset that he simply could not stay in the band any longer. Little Richard had a huge ego, and Jimi wanted the chance to be free: to play his own solos, to wear what he wanted, and not to have a band leader that was mean.

At this point in his early musical career, Jimi Hendrix decided that it was time for a name change; this is popular with a lot of celebrities. They will often change their name, because they think something else sounds cooler. For example, the singer Gotye, whose most popular song was the 2011 hit "Somebody That I Used to Know," does not use his real name: Wouter De Backer. Similarly, the rap singer Jay-Z's real name is Shawn Corey Carter. Even the author of the *Harry Potter* series wrote a new book, under the secret name of Robert Galbraith, though this was because she wanted to see if her writing would be popular if no one knew it was her.

With this in mind, it's not too surprising that Jimi Hendrix temporarily used the name Maurice James when he returned to New York City. He hoped that using a new, cool name might attract more people to his music, as well as give him a fresh start.

Jimi Hendrix soon got a big hit. Whether it was his new stage name or his dedication, we may never know. But the next summer, he was asked to play guitar for a record company, recording with other musicians as well as by himself. Soon after this, he was signed up for a contract with the company PPX Enterprises. Jimi was just starting to make it big!

In terms of his pursuit to find a good band to play with, Jimi still had the same old troubles. It seemed like, no matter where he went, he was not content. Either the band played the same songs over and over again, restricting the amount of creativity Jimi could have, or they were too uptight about their rules. Jimi hopped from band to band, including two called the Squires and the Starliters, and he eventually returned back to the Starliters. As you can see, Jimi had trouble finding solid work.

Eventually, a band called King Curtis and the All-Stars approached him; they wanted him to play! He agreed, mostly because they were about to have an awesome gig at a club in the Harlem Area. King Curtis and the All-Stars were only searching for a temporary player, just someone to fill in for the night. But after the All-Stars saw Jimi Hendrix playing in the club that night, they were stunned; not only that, but the audience in the club was stunned! It turned out that, even if Harlem audiences preferred jazz to rock and roll, Jimi Hendrix could still blow them away with his talent.

King Curtis and the All-Stars immediately hired Jimi Hendrix on full-time, and he was thrilled! He loved the Harlem clubs, and it was here that he would meet someone very important. One night, the All-Stars were performing in a club called the Cheetah Club. In the audience were the regular audience members, but there was also someone else: a woman named Linda Keith from Britain.

Linda Keith was dating a man named Keith Richards, a member of the Rolling Stones (another very famous rock and roll band, made popular for songs such as "Satisfaction," "Jumping Jack Flash," "Beast of Burden," "Under My Thumb," and "Gimme Shelter"). The Rolling Stones had just arrived in New York, where they would be starting a tour of the United States. Linda Keith was eager to visit New York's greatest clubs, of which the Cheetah Club was one. When she saw the All-Stars walk onto the stage, she had no idea what she was about to see.

Overall, she thought the All-Stars were pretty good, but there was one member that stood out above the rest: Jimi Hendrix. Years later, Linda Keith recalled her first experience watching Jimi Hendrix on stage: "The way his hands moved up and down on the neck of the guitar was something to watch. I found myself simply mesmerized by watching him play . . . He was clearly a star, though he was such an odd looking star, and it was such an odd place, it didn't seem right."

But despite that, she knew that she *needed* to talk to Jimi. After the performance, Linda and all of her friends with her invited Jimi Hendrix to their apartment, where they could talk about music. However, it has been said that this is the place where Jimi was also introduced to the drug known as LSD.

For a while, Jimi Hendrix had been into illegal drugs, unfortunately. LSD is an abbreviation for "lysergic acid diethylamide." In the grand classification of drugs, it is referred to as a hallucinogen, meaning that it can make a person see or hear things that are not really there. While most people take it for the "fun" feelings, it can also be severely harmful. It limits brain function and can lead to disaster. LSD is still used today, but it was very popular during Jimi Hendrix's time. If you've ever heard the word "psychedelic," this word became popular because it often described what people saw, heard and felt while they were under the influence of LSD. The drug became so popular, despite the fact it was illegal, that psychedelic came to be a word associated with anything related to the 60s, such as tie-dye and bright colors, and many of the "hippies" that protested the Vietnam War.

Linda, Jimi, and her friends all took LSD, and it was here that Jimi's career started to rev forward. Linda liked Jimi for his crazy clothes, his hair style, his music, and his solos. She saw a lot of potential in him, and it was her gut instinct to talk with him that would eventually change Jimi Hendrix's career and his life.

Chapter 4: The Jimi Hendrix Experience

While people certainly loved Jimi Hendrix, Linda Keith had a very hard time finding any producers that were willing to hire him. Sure, Jimi was extravagant and creative, but would he really appeal to national and international audiences? Linda Keith thought so, but very few other people did. She talked to the producers that worked with the Rolling Stones, but none of them wanted to take the risk. If her own band network wouldn't take on Jimi, then she would have to find someone else.

During the year 1966, Linda Keith found a man by the name of Bryan Chandler. Chandler was in a British band called the Animals, whose most popular song was "House of the Rising Sun." When Linda asked Chandler what he was up to, he told her that he planned to leave playing the bass behind, and instead go into the music producing world. Linda thought that this could be her opportunity to find someone for Jimi! She told him about Jimi Hendrix, a guitar player from the United States who had so much potential, if only he could find the right producer. He agreed.

A month later, Linda and Chandler visited a club called Café Wha?, where Jimi Hendrix was slated to perform. Chandler was very impressed, but he was shocked when Jimi started to play a song called "Hey Joe," which Chandler had been trying to make popular for months. It has been said that he even spilled a milkshake on his suit, he was so surprised to hear Jimi play the song — and he thought Jimi played it perfectly! In the words of Chandler, Jimi Hendrix "was the best guitarist I'd ever seen."

Chandler discussed a contract signing with Jimi, who was on board right away. However, while Jimi made this agreement, there was something that he was forgetting: months ago, Jimi had signed a contract with PPX Enterprises, a contract that restricted him from making deals with other producers. This would become a huge problem later, but for now Jimi would play some gigs in the United States, until Chandler came back to continue their deal.

Just over a month later, Chandler found Jimi Hendrix again. With Chandler came Michael Jeffrey, the manager of the Animals. When Jeffrey first heard Jimi play, he called Jimi a "black Elvis." He wanted to get Jimi Hendrix to England immediately so that they could start some musical work and develop their contract some more.

At first, Jimi was very nervous about going to England; he didn't see the point. He wanted to stay in the United States, where he had a fan base. He thought that England was too small, and they already had a few star guitar players. Among them was Eric Clapton, a jazz musician that Jimi had worshipped for years. Jimi agreed to go to England on one condition: that Chandler would arrange a meeting between him and Clapton. Chandler agreed, and so they were off to London.

Jimi's first night in London was busy. He played at two clubs that night, and got a fantastic reception in both of them. After this, Chandler and Jeffrey decided that if Hendrix was going to remain in London and woo audiences, he would need something larger than a one-person band. So they put out ads, asking for musicians.

The first person that showed genuine interest was a man named Noel Redding. He was twenty years old, and his audition was to play bass while jamming with Jimi Hendrix. Jimi liked him well enough; the band earned its second member.

37

Michael Jeffrey, the manager, realized that the band would need a name. It needed to be something unique and original, something that grabbed an audience's attention and made them want to see more. He eventually came up with "The Jimi Hendrix Experience." He wanted the audience to think that seeing Jimi play was not just a performance, but an "experience."

Meanwhile, while they were searching for more players, Chandler realized that he had an obligation to uphold: Jimi Hendrix needed to meet Eric Clapton. The group attended an Eric Clapton concert. While there, Chandler asked Clapton if Jimi could play with the band. At first, Clapton was a bit unsure; after all, he didn't know who Jimi was. This could be a tremendous waste of time. However, it was the exact opposite.

People who were there said that Eric Clapton's mouth dropped when Jimi started to play. He played at such a fast speed, and his music was so perfectly played. After their short jam session, Eric Clapton was absolutely speechless.

At this point, Jeffrey and Chandler decided that Jimi Hendrix had so much potential, it would be foolish not to start touring him now. They took advantage of a great opportunity, to travel with the singer Johnny Hallyday as he toured around the country of France. The Jimi Hendrix Experience would be the opening band for Hallyday—only there was one small problem. The Jimi Hendrix Experience only had two members in it, and that simply wasn't enough. They needed at least one more player, a drummer, to make a perfect three. Chandler heard of a man named John Mitchell who had just quit a band and was looking for a new gig. Mitchell joined immediately.

Their first performance on tour only lasted for fifteen minutes, but it took place in the amazing Novelty Theatre, in the city of Evreaux, France. Reactions to Jimi Hendrix in France were mixed. Some people thought that he was horrible, that his music was disturbing and horrible to listen to. Other people knew that it was unusual, but they felt that it was a groundbreaking type of music. People often felt this way in the 1800s when listening to composers like Beethoven for the first time. They were unsure of how they felt, but they knew that it was significant, and that it would change the face of the music industry.

In addition to performing in France, the Jimi Hendrix Experience also traveled to Munich, Germany. They performed at a place called the Big Apple Club. While playing on the tour, Jimi Hendrix, to impress the crowd, jumped offstage to play wildly. He threw his guitar back onstage when he was ready, and when he picked it up he realized that he broken the neck of the guitar (the long part). He was so angry that he raised the guitar up in his arms and brought it down on the floor in rage. The guitar smashed and splintered and flew into bits everywhere.

The audience did not know what was wrong, so they just assumed that Jimi Hendrix was pulling some cool new stunt. They cheered and went wild, and thought it was the coolest thing they had ever seen. Jimi Hendrix's famous smashing of the guitar has been replicated through films and even cartoons; it was an iconic moment in the history of rock music, and one that Chandler loved. After the performance, he told Jimi that for other performances, he should smash his guitar since the audience loved it so much.

The tours of France and Germany had made the Jimi Hendrix Experience popular, including a few televised performances. A couple of months later, they realized that it was time to make their first album. During the recording of their album, the band played a song called "Purple Haze," which many people believe to be the Jimi Hendrix Experience's best song ever. While it's hard to tell which of their songs is the *most* famous, there's no doubt that "Purple Haze" would become an instant hit.

The publicity that the Jimi Hendrix Experience suddenly received was astounding. Not only were music fans everywhere talking about the band, but so were very famous musicians. People like Paul McCartney and John Lennon, from the Beatles, were floored by Jimi Hendrix's music. In interviews, sometimes they did nothing but praise Jimi for his music and encourage people to listen to him.

Eventually, the Jimi Hendrix Experience's first album was released, the next spring. It was titled *Are You Experienced*.

The album was an instant hit. People around the world raved about the music performed by the Jimi Hendrix Experience, calling it the future of rock and roll. The members of the band waited anxiously to see where their album would fall on the top hits in Britain. While they did not come in number one, they did come in second place. The number one spot belonged to the Beatles, who had just released the ever-popular *Sgt. Pepper's Lonely Hearts Club Band.* If the Beatles, who were a well-established band, were followed by the brand new Jimi Hendrix Experience, this was a great sign for Jimi. He was instantly rising to the top.

Jimi's managers knew that America must soon experience the popularity of Jimi Hendrix and his band, so they signed a deal to have the album released in the U.S. It was a huge hit, so the Experience decided to tour the United States, something that was exciting for Jimi. It had been a while since he left his home country to become a rock star, and he looking forward to returning.

However, before the band took off for America, they wanted to play a final show so that they could say goodbye to their British fans. They held the show at the Saville Theatre, which was owned by the manager of the Beatles, whose album *Sgt. Pepper's Lonely Hearts Club Band* was taking the country by storm.

42

Jimi Hendrix decided he would perform a tribute to the Beatles by performing their song, "Sgt. Pepper's Lonely Hearts Club Band." The song had only been released three days ago, but Jimi had created an arrangement of the song—all in his head! A half hour before the show started, he went backstage and taught the other members of the Experience the chords to the song, so that they could play it too.

Afterward, people realized that this moment could shatter Jimi Hendrix's career, or propel it forward into fame. If he had played a horrible version of "Sgt. Pepper's Lonely Hearts Club Band," the most popular song in the nation, he easily would have been booed off the stage, and he was playing in the presence of Paul McCartney and George Harrison, no less, two members of the Beatles.

This was not the case, however. The version was fantastic, and Jimi Hendrix was cheered on wildly. Paul McCartney said that listening to Jimi Hendrix perform his song was an absolute "honor." You can find Jimi's version of "Sgt. Pepper's Lonely Hearts Club Band," on YouTube, along with videos of his performance. Of course, Jimi ended his performance that night by lifting his guitar over his head and smashing it on the ground.

After that performance, the Jimi Hendrix Experience took off for the United States. They landed in San Francisco, which Jimi thought was excellent. He had not been there for over five years, since his days in the army. In the time that had passed, San Francisco had become a very different place.

The war in Vietnam had picked up pace. In the five years since Jimi had left San Francisco, a lot had happened to ignite riots and anger from the people: President John F. Kennedy had been assassinated, and each day more and more troops were being dispatched to the far off country of Vietnam, to fight in a senseless war with which America had no right interfering.

Hippy culture had overrun San Francisco. Peace signs could be seen everywhere; drug use was abundant; many people wore their hair long; and protests were a regular event. Many hippies attended the Monterey Pops Festival, one of San Francisco's most popular performances. Several bands came to play here, including the Who, the Mamas and the Papas, the Grateful Dead, and the Jimi Hendrix Experience.

The Experience was one of the last bands to go on, following the Grateful Dead. Many of the people at the event were not very excited to hear the Experience; their popularity was slowly growing, whereas in Britain it had flourished and bloomed. Jimi Hendrix was intent on giving the people a show that would blow their minds away.

As usual, Jimi did not just play music; he *performed*. He swung his guitar behind his back and rattled away on it, he used his teeth to pluck the strings instead of his fingers: all things that the audience had never expected or seen before. To simply amaze the audience, Jimi decided that smashing his guitar just wasn't enough. He needed something more fiery.

During their performance of the song "Wild Thing," Jimi lit his guitar aflame. He then lifted the burning the guitar and smashed it repeatedly. From that point on, no one was ever reluctant to see Jimi Hendrix in concert. After the Monterey Pops Festival, people called this the performance that made America fall in love with Jimi Hendrix.

Michael Jeffrey, the Experience's manager, realized that it was now time to ensure that America could not get enough of Jimi. The band toured through Florida and New York, where the audiences went crazy for the band. *Are You Experienced* became more popular than Frank Sinatra, and one magazine declared that Jimi Hendrix was the "World's Best Pop Musician."

But the Jimi Hendrix Experience was not prepared to slow down by any means. Just as *Are You Experienced* was smashing the top of the charts, they released their next album: *Axis: Bold As Love*. The band returned to England to do a tour for their screaming fans.

This is not to say that the Experience was without its flaws. Every band has its high and low points. The members of the Experience, for instance, used drugs and sometimes tried to compete to see who could intake the most drugs. This obviously created some tension and influenced their minds—and not in a good way. One night, Jimi was arrested for being too disorderly after he became drunk and high in his hotel room. In addition to all of this, their second album *Axis: Bold As Love* was not nearly as popular as *Are You Experienced*. Many people criticized Jimi himself, who then put the blame on other members of the band not letting him get his way.

Despite all the trouble, though, the Experience had another tour to venture on, this one back in the United States. The tour would begin in San Francisco and work its way up to Seattle, Jimi's hometown. He was not nervous about the tour, but he was nervous about meeting his father, who had often disapproved of his style and his music. What would his father say about him now? Amid his rising popularity, he didn't think he could take such a blow to his ego. It would be emotionally devastating to him.

But, in Seattle, when Jimi saw his father for the first time in years, Al did not take a pair of scissors and cut Jimi's wild hair, like he thought he would. Instead, Al hugged Jimi and, reportedly, said the words, "Welcome home, son." It was the best scenario that Jimi could have imagined.

Jimi spent the day at his father's house, where his family was gathered. They were thrilled to see him, even if "was like a hippie," as his Aunt Delores said that day. Jimi was not able to see many of friends, however. Most of them were not in Seattle, but far away in Vietnam.

Jimi played an excellent (and free) performance for the students of Garfield High School, a school he was proud of. This performance was great, despite the fact that he was hungover during it, from a night of drinking with his brother. After the performance, there was a Questions and Answers session that Jimi bombed. Sure, he could play music while he was hungover, but he often said that he felt way too nervous confronting a crowd without a guitar in his hand and music to play. Whatever the reason was, the session went horribly.

Meanwhile, Jimi made a terrific statement on the state of the Vietnam War, something that everyone in the country felt passionately about. To a crowd of people at a concert, he said, "Instead of all that action happening over there, why doesn't everyone just come on home, and instead of M16 machine guns, hand grenades and tanks on their backs, why don't they come back with feedback guitars on their backs? That's better than guns."

The audience cheered. Jimi subscribed to the antiwar sentiment as much as anyone else did; he wanted to, as the modern expression goes, "make beats, not bombs." Another celebrity who supported the antiwar movement was a man named Martin Luther King Jr., who also led the Civil Rights Movement. He wanted equality for African-Americans across America, something that had been denied to them since they were freed from slavery a century earlier. Almost everything was segregated in the south, and he thought it was unfair.

Some people did not agree with Martin Luther King, Jr., and were intent on eliminating him. On April 4th, 1968, a man shot Martin Luther King in Memphis, Tennessee. This death resonated with Jimi Hendrix, being a black man in a country where black and whites were not at all equal. On April 5th, the Jimi Hendrix Experience was supposed to play at Newark Symphony Hall in Newark, New Jersey. There, Jimi Hendrix dedicated a song to the fallen Martin Luther King.

The Experience played a slow, sad, beautiful song. Outside the theater, there were riots in the streets. Civil rights activists and those who sought inequality were clashing. Gunshots sounded. People were injured. But the tribute to Martin Luther King, Jr. went on. When Jimi's concert ended, the audience did not applaud; this was not intended to be rude, but it was out of respect for the solemn atmosphere. Jimi later donated five thousand dollars to a fund for the fallen activist, an amount that equated to about thirty-three thousand dollars today.

But despite the sad events, the Jimi Hendrix Experience failed to come together and overcome their differences. Money was tight among them. They wanted to release a new album, although the band members claimed that Jimi made that difficult, since all he wanted was to experiment. While the other members wanted to record and produce, Jimi just wanted to jam and create new music. Hendrix, on the other hand, thought they were being too uptight about everything.

Amongst this friction, Chandler, the Experience's producer, quit—for a number of reasons. First and foremost, he claimed that Jimi was argumentative and refused to listen to Chandler. Secondly, he was irritated by the screaming, wild fan base that Jimi had accumulated. Sure, it was a great thing for the Experience, but it was not the type of career that Chandler wanted. Thirdly, Chandler kept telling Jimi to cut down on the drugs—which, of course, Jimi did not. He was stubborn and wanted to do things his own way, and he would not listen to anyone who tried to tell him otherwise.

Ultimately, Jimi Hendrix was given a choice: he could either keep Michael Jeffrey or Chandler. Given the friction between Jimi and Chandler, he obviously chose Michael Jeffrey, something that people claimed was a huge mistake. For one thing, Michael Jeffrey was only in the business for one reason: that was money. Chandler, on the other hand, cared about Jimi Hendrix's reputation, which he was worried Jimi would ruin. Chandler never forgave Jimi, but he took off nonetheless, venturing into the next chapter in his life.

As the Experience's next tour of America began, one event occurred that highlights the racial tension of 1960s America, especially in the aftermath of the assassination of Martin Luther King, Jr. The United States was in an uproar. There were shootings left and right; whites and blacks clashed in the streets. More people cried for peaceful protests, while others called for violence. One day, Jimi Hendrix met a white girl (the girl is not actually important; Jimi was known for meeting girls, spending money on them for one day, and then never talking to them again), and they decided to walk together. A police officer saw that Jimi Hendrix (a black man) and the girl (white) were walking together, and aimed his gun at Jimi, instantly assuming that the black man must be terrorizing the white girl.

This event obviously had an impact on Hendrix. When later asked about it, he noted that, "Fifty years ago, I couldn't have even walked into this auditorium. And fifty years from now, no one is going to care." Jimi makes a very astute point; he recognized the horrific racism that plagued the nation at the start of the twentieth century, as well as the progressive views that were taking form. Even though racism still exists today, it is not as prevalent as it was during Jimi Hendrix's time, or even fifty years before that.

As mentioned, not everyone believed in the nonviolence movement supported by activists like Martin Luther King, Jr. and Rosa Parks. There were some groups that believed violence was the only way to enact any sort of change. One of these organizations was called the Black Panthers (who even make an appearance in the popular film *Forrest Gump*). The Black Panthers advocated for a black revolution as the only way to achieve equality. It was a stark contrast to the thought of the pacifist (nonfighting) movement.

Many times, Jimi Hendrix was approached by members of the Black Panthers, asking him to support them. However, Jimi was not one for politics. Of course he supported civil rights and African-American equality, but he thought that he could help out by making music — perhaps, when people saw that an African-American musician was the same as a white musician, they might be less inclined to have racist thoughts.

Jimi Hendrix never openly supported the Black Panthers, although there are some that believe he secretly hoped their violent ways would overcome racist ideologies. Most people, however, think that Jimi was telling the truth when he said that he thought his music could speak louder than violence.

That September, the Jimi Hendrix Experience released their third album, which was called *Electric Ladyland*. On the album was a song called "All Along the Watchtower," which was originally a Bob Dylan song. It was soon the highest-ranking Experience song in the United States. Reviews of the album were almost divided; for one, it had some great music in it, but some critics complained that the album was too long. When faced with these comments, Jimi Hendrix noted that he had hoped the album would be even longer.

Still, the band was being plagued by inner tensions. Jimi Hendrix attributed their problems to their sudden fame; he did not know how difficult it would be to get used to being a pop star. The money, the screaming fans, the popularity—it was overwhelming for the Experience, and this often led to arguments among the band members, Jimi Hendrix most of all.

As a result of their fighting, the Jimi Hendrix Experience never played with the same quality as they had previously. Many of Jimi's biggest fans now thought that he was not playing with the same happiness and devotion that had made him so popular in the first place. Sure, the music was *good*, but it was not the Jimi Hendrix Experience that the world had come to know and love. Jimi was often high when he played on stage, which meant that his playing was messed up and not on target at all.

A few weeks before people started noticing that the Jimi Hendrix Experience was sinking, and sinking fast, Jimi had announced that he had a new girlfriend: her name was Kathy Etchingham. She had attended his concerts, and now he wanted her to join him on their next tour of the United States. Etchingham was originally from the United Kingdom, and had never been to New York before.

The City That Never Sleeps intimidated her; she found it huge and daunting. More than the city, she disliked Jimi Hendrix's entourage of friends that accompanied him everywhere. Jimi was constantly followed by friends, fans that were wild supporters, his producers, businessmen, and people who were into drugs. Jimi always wanted a supply of drugs close by, so he was usually followed by someone who was ready to sell him some.

Needless to say, Kathy Etchingham did not like this one bit, but the tipping point was discovering that one of the drug-dealers was packing a gun 24/7. She told Hendrix that she was leaving New York to return to England, and that they could no longer be together. In the end, Jimi Hendrix could not give Kathy Etchingham what she wanted: a stable life. Jimi was too stubborn, unpredictable, and lived too much in the moment. Kathy, on the other hand, wanted to settle down with a family. Jimi had other plans. Little did Jimi Hendrix and Kathy Etchingham know that the drug problem would soon escalate past the point of no return.

As the band flew into Canada, their bags were checked and searched. Inside, the Canadian police found heroin, an illegal drug. Jimi Hendrix was arrested on the spot.

This news could easily have instantly exploded across the world, while a man named Michael Goldstein, who worked as Jimi Hendrix's public relations man, decided he had to keep this story off the press. He went down to the Associated Press and gave the editor there some alcohol, in return for not covering the story. And so, it would be a while before anyone found out about Jimi Hendrix's arrest and the inconveniences that faced the Experience.

The police held Jimi at a ten thousand dollar bail, which he paid himself so that he could go to a concert that night in Toronto. Even though he paid the bail, however, he would still have to face the courts yet again.

It was this concert that made Jimi Hendrix's face skyrocket in Canada. It made him the rock star with the highest salary — not just in North America, but in the entire world. After Toronto, the Jimi Hendrix Experience moved onto Seattle, Jimi's hometown, and then to Los Angeles, California.

It was in Los Angeles that the Jimi Hendrix Experience had an interview with *Rolling Stone* magazine, which covers music news and celebrities. During the interview, Jimi Hendrix mentioned that he was about to go on a tour with another band — the other members of the Experience were just as surprised to hear this as the interviewer was. This was the first time Jimi had mentioned anything about touring with another group. The other members saw it as insulting, that Jimi would keep something like this from them. But then again, many people questioned whether Jimi was telling to the truth. He also denied any rumors that the Experience was about to break up.

From here, it was all downhill. None of the Experience's shows were the same. Some historians claim that Jimi Hendrix's tension and stress because of his impending court trial caused him to be testy, stubborn, and angry. Whatever the cause of the friction among the group members, the concerts went horribly. The band members squabbled on stage, and Jimi even ended up swearing at his paying audience members.

The Jimi Hendrix Experience arrived in Denver, Colorado to perform at the Denver Pop Festival, a much anticipated event. It was here that the Experience would fall apart.

Outside Mile High Stadium, fans were rioting: they wanted free admission to the concert, because the tickets were way too expensive. Jimi Hendrix walked by some of the angry fans outside and exchanged words with them. He announced, very suddenly, that their performance at Mile High Stadium would be their last.

This only incited the fans' anger. They tried to ambush the stage, and the police responded likewise — with tear gas. The Experience managed to escape the furious crowds, but they could not escape the inevitable truth: they would never play together again. Hendrix immediately departed Denver and left for New York, angry at his band members, his fans, and the world.

Chapter 5: Woodstock

The Experience had been an enormous part of Jimi's life for years; it was the reason he went from some guitarist at jazz clubs to the world's number one rocker. He still kept in touch with Mitchell, the drummer, who had often tried to defuse the Experience's arguments.

With Jimi Hendrix's court case looming overhead like a rain cloud, he realized he needed to find some way to make some more money, and he also wanted to make some more music. With Mitchell still by his side, Jimi made a phone call to his friend from the army, Billy Cox, whom he had not seen in ages. Also in the meanwhile, Jimi was trying to find himself a girlfriend.

Since things had fallen out with Kathy Etchingham in New York City, Jimi had drifted from girl to girl, as had often been his style. Many of his girlfriends had no deep love for him, though—they were infatuated with his status, but even more than that, they loved him for his *music*.

Jimi Hendrix landed a place in the town of Shokan, New York, a rural area that was a stark contrast to New York City. The house, however, was huge. It had eight bedrooms, had a pool in the backyard, and was staffed with a chef and housekeeper. In today's money, the house cost $16,000 per month, a tremendous amount compared to other house or apartment costs.

After he settled into his new home, Jimi Hendrix turned towards repairing his broken career. He was still getting money from record sales, but without the rest of the Experience to turn out new albums, the money would not be coming in forever. And that was when he realized he should make a new album—perhaps with new band members. He wanted to create a bigger band, something he had advocated from the start.

Jimi hired a few people from around the country, who eagerly accepted the invitation to join a project spearheaded by Jimi Hendrix. There was Billy Cox, Juma Sultan, Jerry Velez, and Larry Lee for the new band; Jimi was still unsure whether Mitch Mitchell would be joining the new group. All of these men moved into Jimi Hendrix's eight-bedroom house, where they could spend most of their time trying to make good music.

It was then that Jimi Hendrix would be part of an experience that would shape American culture forever. The event is called Woodstock, and it defined the 1960s and 1970s, mainly because it was a flocking area for hippie culture and anti-war sentiment. Jimi Hendrix was thrilled to play at Woodstock, since the crowd was huge and publicity was incredible. That year, when people talked about Woodstock, the topic of conversation was Jimi Hendrix, and how he would perform after the falling out of the Experience.

But before the band played at Woodstock, Jimi realized that they desperately needed a drummer. Mitch Mitchell came back to fill the role, although he was nervous about being in a band with Jimi Hendrix again. Despite being friends with Jimi, he did recognize that Jimi's stubbornness and temper had caused a lot of problems during the age of the Experience.

Woodstock was meant to be great that year. Amidst Jimi Hendrix and his group of musicians (who were unnamed as of yet), there would be the Grateful Dead, the Who, Sly and the Family Stone, Nash and Young, Santana, and Janis Joplin.

When the event started, *eight hundred thousand* people showed up to attend. That was the breaking point for attendance. There were two hundred thousand other people that tried to show up at the concert, but there was simply no room for them. Woodstock, which took place over a few days (especially since the concert was so far behind schedule) was not as populated when Jimi Hendrix finally arrived. In fact, the numbers had dwindled from eight hundred thousand to forty-three thousand.

They had a morning performance, but when they stepped onto the stage, the announcer had no idea what to call the band. Thinking on his feet, he introduced them as the Jimi Hendrix Experience. Jimi quickly corrected him and said that the band would no longer be called the Experience, but instead, "Gypsy, Sun, and Rainbows." It was a decision that he had thought about for a while, and he thought the name fit perfectly with hippie culture.

The band was not prepared for the long performance ahead of them, which was slated to last two hours. They had not rehearsed enough. Jimi decided that they could just jam and make stuff up as they go. This was evidently not what the audience wanted to hear, so many people decided to up and leave.

That was when Jimi had a brilliant idea. The sunrise was just happening, and he thought it would be a great idea to welcome the new day with the Star-Spangled Banner. Combining the classical excellence of Francis Scott Key's composition with the modern twist of Jimi Hendrix stunned the crowd—in a good way. Jimi even imitated bomb explosions on his guitar to make the song more dramatic.

A reporter for the *New York Times* would later declare that "It was the most electrifying moment of Woodstock, and it was the single greatest moment of the sixties. You finally heard what that was about, that you can love your country, but hate the government."

This reporter makes an excellent point. Many people at the time were disappointed with the United States government, mostly because of how they were handling the war in Vietnam. Every day, more American soldiers were reported dead or missing in Vietnam, and the public was fed up. They wanted the war to end, although the government was not listening. The people wanted to love and have faith in their country and people, but not in the government. Jimi Hendrix, as he played the National Anthem at a hippie festival, inspired this idea.

Jimi Hendrix never meant for it to be this way. He just wanted to play a song that united all of his listeners; he never thought that his audience would interpret as anti-war or anti-government. He wrapped up his performance by playing "Hey Joe," and that was the end of it. Jimi Hendrix left Woodstock, a hotbed of discussion in his wake.

Chapter 6: Band of Gypsys

With Woodstock, one of the biggest performances of Hendrix's life, over, Gypsy, Sun, and Rainbows had new plans on their mind. They continued to jam and play, as Jimi had always wanted in his previous bands, and occasionally pumped out a few tracks. None skyrocketed to fame as his songs did during the Experience era, but Jimi kept his name out there.

Gypsy, Sun, and Rainbows did not last too much longer. After a complete failure of a show in Harlem, New York, the band decided to throw their towels in and go their separate ways. But Jimi Hendrix hardly had time to think about forming a new band. There was much else on his mind.

It was at this time, all these months later, that Jimi Hendrix finally went on trial for being caught with drugs at the Toronto Airport long ago. The trial took place in Toronto, Canada.

Jimi had a very difficult case to battle. The Canadian police knew that the drugs had been in Jimi's bags, so there wasn't much he could say to deny it. His lawyer claimed that some of Jimi's fans had given him the heroin, and that Jimi had no idea it had been accidentally thrown into his luggage. This was obviously a lie, and not the first one that would be told during the trial.

In order to get a better idea of Jimi's drug history, and hence the likelihood that he might be carrying heroin with him, the court asked Jimi about his previous drug use. Despite having used drugs severely over the years, beginning when he was a teenager, Jimi claimed that he had only used drugs including cocaine and LSD a few times—this was far from the truth. To make the courts believe him, he said that he, in the recent past, had smoked marijuana, but *never* done heroin, the drug found in his bag. He thought that if he admitted to drug use, but not the drugs with which he was caught, the courts might let him off easy.

After recounting numerous instances in which fans may have given him drugs, and he received them unknowingly, the jury ultimately decided that Jimi Hendrix was not guilty. This trial did not impact Jimi's drug use; he continued to use, even if he knew he might get caught again.

Now that he was free of possible jail time, Jimi decided to get back into music and form a new band. Perhaps, he thought, this time he would not have so many players. He decided on three: the magic number of the Experience. Billy Cox was in the band, and so was a man named Buddy Miles, who played the drums. They decided to call themselves the Band of Gypsys.

The Band of Gypsys did not start out too hot. Their first official performance was at The Fillmore East in New York City, and it was a flop. The audience did not like their music; some booed, while others walked out in annoyance.

The failed performance made Jimi angry, and also motivated him to do much better the next time. Their next performance was in the same theatre, and Jimi was intent on rocking on and stunning the audience—which is exactly what happened. Jimi was a musician who played much better when he was allowed to jam and play what he wanted, as opposed to following music.

A man from the *New York Times* claimed that Jimi Hendrix "seems to be more concerned with creating an environment of intense sound and personal fury than he is with performing a particular composition. Jimi Hendrix playing a Jimi Hendrix song is one of the least-understandable performers to someone who is not a full-blown rock follower. He really is a piece of underground scenery, and has to be appreciated as such."

Sometimes, the best musicians are the strangest ones, and Jimi's jam sessions were certainly strange. He had a way with music; only, it was a way that many people, and musicians, were not familiar with.

After they rocked that performance, the Band of Gypsys decided to perform at Madison Square Garden in New York, at an event called the "Winter Festival for Peace." The show went great at first, but then it went downhill. Jimi was pale and shaking, and eventually he had to sit down on stage—in the middle of the performance! Most people wondered if he was sick, or even if he going to die. But the likely answer behind Jimi's sudden sickness is the drugs he was taking.

It might have been an overdose of LSD, or even some unknown drug thrown into his food or drink. Nevertheless, he was fine the next day. While he was not permanently impacted by the event, many people wondered whether his incessant drug use was getting the better of him.

This was the end for the Band of Gypsys. Each member went his own separate way — or at least, that was the original plan. The world was shocked when Jimi soon unveiled a new plan: he was going to get the Jimi Hendrix Experience rolling again.

Chapter 7: Cry of Love Tour

Jimi called Noel Redding and Mitch Mitchell, the original members of the Experience, back to New York to meet with him. The world was abuzz: would the Experience actually get back together? Would they make excellent music like they did before?

Sadly, things would never be the same. Jimi made the decision to cut Noel Redding from the Experience—perhaps because Jimi and Noel never stopped feuding during the era of the Experience. Noel Redding was instead replaced with Billy Cox.

The new band—Jimi Hendrix, Mitch Mitchell, and Billy Cox—were called by a couple of different names. Some people called them the Experience, wishing for the good ol' days when Jimi Hendrix took the globe by storm with his music. Other people called them the Cry of Love, a name that had been floating around for a while.

No matter what you called them, Jimi Hendrix was ready to make his great return. Jimi was intent on recording immediately and starting a tour of the United States. They began in Los Angeles, one of Jimi's favorite places to perform. Jimi wanted to start playing some new tunes, but unfortunately, that was not what his audience wanted.

Perhaps it was because Hendrix fans were nostalgic for the days of the Experience, but they wanted to hear the popular songs from years ago. That was not what Hendrix wanted, however. He was constantly writing new music and experimenting with new riffs.

The Cry of Love Tour was punctuated with riots and upset fans. As had happened before, many of them wanted to be let in for free; the tickets were simply too expensive. The police were needed to beat unruly fans back and protect Jimi.

Despite all of the chaos, Jimi still managed to put on some great shows; the fans that *did* get in and see him perform loved it. The whole summer was a season of excellent shows, and even pumping out a few songs. There was July 4th performance, where Jimi did his famous rendition of the Star-Spangled Banner, and another show at the New York Pop Festival.

Their tour of the U.S. also included Jimi's hometown of Seattle. None of his shows here went too well. Part of the reason was because Jimi was tired and weary, possibly because of all the drugs he was ingesting. His motivation sank, and so did his talent. He got angry very easily at his fans, swearing and giving the middle finger when someone threw a pillow for him to autograph on stage.

Normally, after the show, fans would cheer for an encore; but at this final show in Seattle, there would be no encore for Jimi. He walked off the stage, his fans left, and that was the end of it. Just as he left the stage with a sour taste in his mouth, so, too, did he leave his father. They got into a silly argument, but Jimi had no chance to make it up; he was now on a plane to Hawaii, where the Cry of Love would finish their American tour.

In Hawaii, he was unable to get heroin, which made Jimi angry and upset. Because of this, he took increased dosages of LSD, marijuana, and cocaine. The Cry of Love played from Maui to Honolulu, and they thought Hawaii was an absolutely gorgeous place to stay. After the tour had officially ended, Billy Cox and Mitch Mitchell flew back to the continental U.S., while Jimi decided to stay on a vacation.

During his Hawaiian vacation, he wrote music and lyrics, hoping to take his mind off his heroin withdrawals and his numerous money problems. He ended his vacation by writing an apologetic letter to his father, saying sorry for the pointless argument they had before Jimi left Seattle.

Chapter 8: Electric Lady Studios

Since the days of the Jimi Hendrix Experience, Jimi had not been using a normal record company. At the time of building the Experience, Jimi and Michael Jeffrey knew that using any company would cost a lot of money, which they just didn't have. However, they realized that if they created their *own* company, they would not pay as much.

With that, Electric Lady Studios was born, named after the Experience's album *Electric Ladyland*. Electric Lady Studios was created as an attempt to save the Experience some money, and it would later become much more. The studio produced almost all of Jimi Hendrix's songs, well past the years of the Experience. Both Michael Jeffrey and Jimi Hendrix co-managed Electric Lady Studios, something that put Jimi into a fascinating position.

At that time, not many African-Americans were famous musicians, never mind musicians that managed a production studio. It was something that Jimi would be forever proud of, something that he could call his own. Despite many odds that faced him while he was young, Jimi had overcome all, become one of the most successful musicians in the world, and co-owned a music studio. There could hardly be anything better.

In August of 1970, Jimi Hendrix and Michael Jeffrey planned an official "opening" of Electric Lady Studios, despite the fact that the studio had been in operation for years. They realized that Electric Lady Studios could take on other musicians and other bands, increasing their profit and popularizing their name.

August 26th was the official opening day, and it was planned to be a day of great success and celebration. However, like many of Jimi's final concerts, things did not go exactly as planned. Many of the guests were out-of-their-mind drunk and high; property was destroyed; and things got out of control. Jimi himself could not even take the party. He checked out early, sick of it.

Jimi also realized that he *needed* to stop using drugs. As one of Jimi's childhood friends once said, "He was over the line. He was aware that it was hurting him. He was making efforts, but somehow, through management or someone, people were always funneling drugs to him."

One of Jimi's suppliers was a girl named Devon Wilson, one of Jimi's old friends. She had always been into drugs, and was normally on hand to deliver whatever Jimi wanted to him. But in August, Jimi put his foot down. Enough was enough. Even though Wilson insisted that Jimi purchase drugs from her, Jimi declined. He needed to get clean, or else it could be his life on the line.

Unfortunately for Jimi, it was too little, too late. He had been using drugs for years, and the effects got to him before he could stop it.

Chapter 9: European Tour

The final weeks of Jimi Hendrix's life were turbulent and troublesome.

After the opening of Electric Lady Studios, Jimi decided to venture back to Europe. He wanted to do another musical tour, and he had found way too much criticism and riotous fans in the United States. He missed England, where his fame had first skyrocketed.

While the Cry of Love did not last too long (none of Jimi's bands seemed to), he was intent on turning his life around and continuing what he always wanted to do: play music. Upon his arrival in the United Kingdom, Jimi said in an interview:

"It's all turned full circle; I'm back right now where I started. I've given this ear of music everything. I still sound the same, my music's the same, and I can't think of anything new to add to it in its present state. Something new has got to come, and Jimi Hendrix will be there. I want a big band . . . full of competent musicians that I can conduct and write for. And with the music we will paint pictures of earth and space, so that the listener can be taken somewhere . . . I don't any longer dig the pop and politics crap. That's old fashioned. . . . When there are vast changes in the way the world goes, it's usually something like art and music that changes it. Music is going to change the world next time."

These words are perfectly emblematic of what Jimi Hendrix stood for, and what he wanted to do in life. Even though some people viewed him as a symbol for racial empowerment or political gain, he only saw one thing: music.

His first performance in England was at the Isle of Wight Festival, which attracted over six hundred thousand screaming fans. The performance was riddled with errors. The schedule was hours behind, the fans were rioting and demanding free access, and Jimi's guitar amplifier kept on breaking. And to make things worse, he ripped the crotch area of his pants. The show ended with fans throwing fiery objects onto the stage; the police immediately set about containing the fire and beating back the rioting audience. Jimi Hendrix was rushed off stage, and the next step in his tour began.

His plane landed next in Stockholm, the capital of Sweden, where a woman met Hendrix and claimed that she had carried his child. Billy Cox was drugged by an unknown person, and got incredibly high and paranoid. Everything that could go wrong *did* go wrong, including Jimi Hendrix ingesting numerous sleeping pills to help take away his stress. At his next concert, he collapsed on stage, and all the fans went home angry and disappointed.

Jimi probably should have stopped his tour. He was weak and his mind was not in the right place. But he continued on to Berlin, where his performances were plagued with trouble and angry fans.

When the European Tour finally ended in London, Jimi went under the radar. he had told his managers he wanted to take a break from music for two years, but hardly anyone believed that—not coming from Jimi Hendrix! Nevertheless, the stress became so bad that Jimi decided to leave.

Very few people saw him after the European Tour ended. One of the people who did was Kathy Etchingham, Jimi's old girlfriend who left him after a disastrous trip to New York City. Etchingham noted that Jimi was hanging out with a blonde woman whom she had never seen before. Another person who saw Jimi Hendrix was Linda Keith, the English woman who first saw Jimi playing in a nightclub and decided to bring him to London. Linda Keith also reported seeing Jimi with the blonde woman. So who was she?

Her name was Monika Danneman, and she was an ice skater from Germany. Danneman later said that she and Jimi had been friends over the years, although historians can barely find any record of the two of them maintaining contact. Nevertheless, the whole world was very confused about Jimi's relationship with this mysterious Danneman. For one thing, whenever Jimi was sighted, he looked absolutely horrible. He looked pale and sick, exhausted beyond belief. Someone also reported hearing Danneman refer to herself as Jimi's fiancée. No one is exactly sure what happened to Jimi during his final days; it was a maelstrom of confusion due to his disappearance and his over-the-top drug usage.

What historians do know, is that on September 17th, Jimi Hendrix met up with Devon Wilson, his former drug supplier. Hendrix, Wilson, and Danneman smoked hash, and Hendrix left with Danneman sometime around three in the morning the next day.

Hendrix and Danneman went to sleep together, each of them taking numerous sleeping pills. On top of the pills, Jimi had been smoking drugs and drinking wine. In the early morning hours, he woke up while Danneman was still asleep and found more of her sleeping pills. Her pills came from Germany and were produced *very* strongly — something that Hendrix did not know about.

He ingested nine of the pills — *twenty times* what doctors recommend, according to Jimi's size. He immediately fell asleep, knocked out. During the course of his sleep, his body vomited. Since he was asleep, however, he could not clean out his mouth and throat. Eventually he stopped breathing and promptly died.

When Danneman finally awoke, she was in a frenzy — imagine waking up and finding that one of the world's most famous celebrities has died in your bed, on your watch.

There is some controversy surrounding Jimi's death. One of Jimi's friends, Eric Burdon, was on the scene as soon as Danneman called him, panicking. When he arrived, he found a song that Jimi had written the night before, called "The Story of Life." The lyrics, which you can look up online, appeared to Burdon like a suicide note. He immediately declared that Jimi had committed a suicide, something that many people still believe.

As one can imagine, Jimi's father Al was devastated when he heard the news. Al inherited all of Jimi's money and belongings, since Jimi had no wife and no children. He was only twenty-seven when he died, something that made his death that more tragic.

Jimi Hendrix was buried on October 1st in Seattle. Over two hundred people attended his funeral; among them were his father, Al; Noel Redding; Mitch Mitchell; Miles Davis, the famous trumpeter of jazz legend; and all of his friends and family. A musical tribute was held in the Seattle Center House, where Noel Redding and Mitch Mitchell jammed together in honor of their friend; they found it difficult, however, to now play without Hendrix.

Chapter 10: Legacy

Despite having died over forty years ago, Jimi Hendrix remains one of the most influential and popular guitarists to have ever lived. His music is still listened to today, and music magazines still point to him as an example of a fantastic musician. The music magazine *Rolling Stone* listed Jimi Hendrix as the number one greatest guitarist of all time.

More than just influencing the world of the guitar, Jimi popularized the *electric* guitar, an instrument that raced ahead to fame with Jimi Hendrix. Both are still used today, but many people theorize that the electric guitar would not be as popular if Jimi Hendrix had not made it so.

While many of his songs are not that memorable and popular today, Jimi is mostly remembered for his innovation. He was not afraid to experiment and try a new piece of music; the greatest examples are the fact that he sometimes played the guitar with his teeth, smashing his guitar, and even lighting his guitar on fire. Very few, if any, musicians would have had that sort of idea, never mind the bravery to do it in front of a screaming audience.

Jimi inspired numerous musicians that came after him. Chief among them was Prince, who used an electric guitar and also played rock & roll. Even the bands at the time, such as the Rolling Stones, the Who, and the Grateful Dead, marveled at Jimi's playing and the ease with which he attracted fans across the globe.

One of the reasons that so many people followed Jimi was not because of his excellent playing — not his lyrics or his crazy outfits and the guitar smashing. Rather, they followed him because of his emotion and the feeling that he delivered. He made people feel good. Through the power of music, he connected people everywhere.

The story of Jimi Hendrix is a sad one. He was a fantastic musician whose life was destroyed by the attraction of drugs. Had Jimi never overdosed or spent much of time stumbling around high, it is impossible to tell what wonders of music he may have worked later in his life. All we can do now is study the man, the myth, the legend, who changed the face of rock and roll and inspired people around the globe to pick up their first guitar.

Jimi Hendrix left for us a legacy that instructs us to love music, because music is a universal language. It transcends languages and even time, which is why we still love and listen to Jimi Hendrix today.

Works Cited

Cross, Charles R. *Room Full of Mirrors: A Biography of Jimi Hendrix*. New York: Hyperion, 2005.

Lawrence, Sharon. *Jimi Hendrix: The Man, the Magic, the Truth*. New York: HarperEntertainment, 2005.

Potash, Crish, ed. *The Jimi Hendrix Companion: Three Decades of Commentary*. New York: Schirmer Books, 1996.

Shapiro, Harry, and Caesar Glebbeek. *Jimi Hendrix: Electric Gypsy*. New York: St. Martin's Griffin, 1995.

Willett, Edward. *Jimi Hendrix: "Kiss the Sky."* Berkeley Heights: Enslow Publishers, 2006.

http://www.musicfanclubs.org/jimihendrix

http://www.jimihendrixmemorial.com

http://www.jimi-hendrix.com

http://www.biography.com/people/jimi-hendrix-9334756

http://www.allmusic.com/artist/jimi-hendrix-mn0000354105/biography

Printed in Great Britain
by Amazon